CAMPING HORROR STORIES

VOLUME 2

Compiled and edited by

Tom Lyons

&

Steven Armstrong

CAMPING HORROR STORIES,
VOLUME 2

All information and opinions expressed
in *Camping Horror Stories, Volume 2*
are based upon the personal
perspectives and experiences of those
generous enough to submit them. The
authors do not purport that the
information presented in this book is
based on accurate, current, or valid
scientific knowledge.

Acknowledgments

It's no easy task for people to discuss their encounters with cryptids. I want to thank the many good people who took the time and energy to put their experiences into writing.

Some of the following names were altered to protect people's privacy.

Would you like to see your report in an issue of *Camping Horror Stories*?

If so, all you have to do is type up a summary of your experience and email it to Tom Lyons at:

Living.Among.Bigfoot@gmail.com

Special Offer

If you submit a report and it is accepted, you will receive an exclusive paperback copy signed by Tom shortly after the book is released. If you'd like to participate in that offer, please include your mailing address in the Email.

Contents

Report #1

Hello. I'm Amanda, and I had an experience a long time ago that I think would be perfect for one of your books. In the early 90s, my stepdad, Ben, took my brother, Tommy, and me on a camping trip in Maine. Tommy was in his early teenage years and seemed to refuse to get along with the man who had recently married our mother. I had difficulty understanding why, for I thought Ben was the nicest guy. My brother's hormones were probably raging at the time, so I think he was going through a bit of a defiant stage. He always argued with our mom and couldn't refrain from blaming her for disrupting her marriage with our biological father. I suppose they thought we were too young to know all the details about why they separated, but I wish we did because I think Tommy would have been easier on her then.

Ben was exceptionally patient with my brother, and I remember him mentioning how he behaved the same way as a youngster. He didn't seem to take any of Tommy's verbal abuse or disrespect personally, which genuinely impressed me, even when I was twelve. Amazingly, the man would blame himself, stating that it was his fault that Tommy didn't like him much and that he needed to put more time toward building a positive relationship with his stepkids. Since we were nearing the end of the summer, Ben thought it would be a good idea to take us on a camping trip in Maine. We lived in New Hampshire, so it wasn't a long drive to where he wanted to take us.

He took us to a "secret' location called Birch Point Beach. Upon arrival, we learned that we weren't allowed to camp there, but Ben assured me that he got away with it on many occasions with his father back in the day. I bet it would be trickier to do without getting in trouble nowadays, for society has been unnecessarily strict on so many fronts since the 90s. Everyone's always so worried about lawsuits, so I wouldn't be surprised if they now have security patrolling the area twenty-four hours daily.

Upon arrival, the first thing we did was gather firewood. Ben said it was always a good idea to do that as soon as you arrive at the campsite, for you wanted to look for the best wood while it was still light outside. I remember he also joked about how doing so would give us the best chance of avoiding predators lurking in the darkness. In some ways, that was almost a form of foreshadowing.

The three of us went swimming as soon as we finished gathering wood. The water was so cold, as is almost always the case in the northeast, no matter the time of year, and I remember pondering how crazy it seemed that aquatic mammals didn't mind that temperature. I recall having this ominous feeling that something unusual was lurking beneath the surface nearby, but I dismissed it, given it's common for people to feel that way when in the ocean.

I figured it was just my instincts reminding me how vulnerable humans are in the water, so I didn't think too deeply about it. I also didn't want to come off as scared, for Tommy always made fun of me for being a wimp. So, I wasn't about to give him plenty of fuel to mock me by alerting him and our stepfather that I thought something strange might be in the water.

The day was a lot of fun, and Tommy even seemed to be opening up more toward Ben. It was as if Ben knew what he needed to do to get my brother to warm up to him. He even discussed planning several more camping trips before summer ended.

The day became even more exciting when Ben revealed that he had purchased an inflatable raft for our trip. It was one of those heavy-duty ones that could fit four people.

He told us we would take it out in the morning if the ocean were calm. My brother had a thing for boats, so he was ecstatic over that idea.

A few hours after we went to bed, I heard someone unzipping the tent. It was Tommy, and he was on his way outside to pee. Ben sounded half asleep when he requested that my brother not wander too far off, especially considering he didn't have a flashlight. Things seemed perfectly calm until I heard my brother scream from a distance. Immediately, I knew he had encountered someone or something dangerous. Ben bolted out of the tent before we could exchange a word.

I was so worried about my brother that I didn't even consider how afraid I was of his startling yelp. I'm guessing it was because I felt safe with our stepdad around, for he was a pretty athletic guy. When you're a little kid, You tend to think that every grown man can protect you from whatever is out there.

Only a few moments after I stepped outside the tent, I noticed the small dog-sized bodies scurrying about the sand. Most headed in the same direction, and I quickly ascertained that it was likely my brother's location they were moving toward. It was too dark outside to tell what they were. All I could see was that they all had tails that were maybe a foot long.

Again, the thought of my brother getting swarmed by whatever these things were was too much to bear, so I tried to keep my distance while running in the same direction they were going. As far as I could hear, they didn't make any noise other than what came from them dragging their torsos along the sand.

As expected, I soon spotted the creatures heading toward the silhouettes that could only belong to a man and a teenage boy. Instead of shouting, Ben preserved his energy while guarding my brother, fully prepared to kick the first creature that pounced. Although none of them seemed to have yet lunged at my family members, it wasn't long before

I realized the animals were circling them, and that circle was steadily tightening.

"Amanda, get to the car now!" Ben hollered once he spotted me.

"But—but—I—," I stuttered.

"Now!" he interrupted before I could find the words to finish my sentence. I had never heard Ben yell like that before, which helped reaffirm that we were dealing with a dire situation.

"The car's unlocked," Ben added while keeping his eyes on the four-legged creatures. "Get in and lock the doors until you hear us coming."

I did as the man instructed. Fortunately, I didn't encounter any of the mysterious animals on the way to the vehicle. After I got inside, I immediately started growing more anxious by the second. I had no light source to see far beyond the windshield, so I couldn't tell if my loved ones were coming to meet me. I was too young to understand how to turn on the headlights, and I wasn't even sure whether I could without the car keys. I climbed into the backseat, figuring our escape would be quicker if I left the front seats available for Ben and my brother.

The vehicle's interior muffled the noise from the creatures' steps, so I couldn't detect if some of them had decided to head to my location. As I sat there, praying that Ben and

Tommy would arrive unharmed the next moment, the reality that I was living through a real-life nightmare became utterly overwhelming.

I nearly fainted when the car's passenger side door suddenly swung open. But the gratitude from spotting my stepdad and brother soon overpowered my startled reaction. However, a new disturbing sight soon caught my eye, and my nerves returned full force. Though I wasn't exactly sure where it came from, my brother was bleeding. And at first glance, it appeared pretty bad. Ben had already removed his white tee shirt and was holding it against my brother's wound, which seemed to be alongside his right hip.

"What happened?" I cried, already having a pretty good idea regarding the answer.

"One of those animals attacked him while he was peeing," Ben said, focused on trying to suppress the bleeding rather than immediately satisfy my curiosity.

"Amanda, I need you to help press this shirt against your brother's wound and hold it there until we get to a hospital."

I nodded without saying anything.

Right after Ben helped Tommy climb into the backseat with me, he turned on the ignition and the high-beam headlights. I couldn't help but scream when I saw the swarm of creatures. They were incomprehensibly ugly, and there were so many of them.

I only glimpsed them briefly before Ben stepped on the gas and got us out of there, but the simplest way to describe them would be to say they looked like pale snapping turtles without shells. I'm unsure how accurate that description is, for I was terrified beyond belief, but that's the best I can do for the sake of this report.

After that brief horrifying glimpse ended, I experienced the sensation of driving over one creature after another. I couldn't believe how many had followed Ben and Tommy to the car. It was the bumpiest ride of my life. It seemed we drove over many more creatures than I had seen through the headlights. Fortunately, it wasn't long before we arrived on the road, and the drive became smooth. I then put all my attention toward tending to my brother's wound.

Everything after that is a blur. I remember being at the emergency room much less vividly than the previous terror. That probably related to how I imagined the worst-case scenarios about my brother's outcome. I was so young, so inexperienced, having no idea whether Tommy had suffered a life-ending injury. Fortunately, he ended up being okay. He received a rabies shot, which, if I recall correctly, was administered through his stomach. I remember feeling queasy over just the idea of having a needle penetrate the abdomen. That was the time I discovered they did stuff like that. That almost sounded like a worse nightmare than what we went through before heading for the hospital.

Ben seemed to be under the impression that the police, animal control, or some other kind of specialists were planning to investigate the scene of the mysterious happening, hoping they could capture one of the creatures. But nobody ever updated him on the matter. He probably thought that, at the very least, someone would recover one of the bodies we had driven over on our way out of the campsite.

That upset the guy, and he grew even more frustrated when he returned to the scene a few days later and found no trace of what happened. Being so young, I didn't know what to think of that whole thing. I assumed someone had to have confused the contact information, or the creatures had left the area, and scavengers quickly disposed of the corpses. These days, I suspect there was something much more covert at play, and someone intended to suppress any findings regarding everything about what occurred during our camping trip.

Years later, my husband brought up something about a growing problem with an invasive species known as snakehead fish. According to him, there was news of them negatively impacting our ecosystems. I felt excited when he informed me of the issue, thinking I would finally get some answers regarding what I went through so many years ago.

Unfortunately, I knew that wasn't what had attacked my brother when I saw the photographs. Although snakeheads can move about the land, they don't have feet and aren't nearly as efficient out of water. Whatever we encountered that night appeared to have well-developed limbs, much like an amphibian. Annoyingly, my husband has concluded that it must've been a snakehead that bit my brother, and we've even gotten into some pretty nasty arguments over it. I can't be sure, but I'm confident it had to be some species of cryptid that chased us all those years ago.

But I will admit there's always the chance it was merely some undiscovered amphibian. After reading so many of your books, Mr. Lyons, I doubt I will ever know the truth of that traumatic event. In any case, thank you for trying to bring more attention to unexplained happenings.

Report #2

Hello. I'm contacting you because I experienced something I would like to get off my chest. I've wanted to talk about it with someone who will genuinely listen. After poking around on the web, I figured that you, Tom, would like to learn what I, along with a few friends, went through one night in Vermont.

I would rather not disclose my identity, for I come from a small town where rumors spread fast. Growing up in Marlboro, I learned your peers won't hesitate to make up the nastiest things about you. Unfortunately, that's been happening to me since high school, and it doesn't seem to be slowing down. The last thing I need is to give anyone more ammunition.

If those numskulls ever discovered that I had submitted a report to a Bigfoot-related publication, everyone around me would know instantly, and I would never hear the end of it. That must sound thin-skinned of me to care, but if you come from a small town, you probably empathize when I say it's best to avoid giving people more fuel for the fire. Many perceived me as one of the prettier girls in my school, which seemed to anger many of my female class members.

There's a famous landmark near where I'm from called Hogback Mountain. Once upon a time, it was a popular place to ski, but I believe they closed that business in the 80s. Nowadays, it's known for its expansive views, so it's an excellent location for hiking. It's a beautiful but also ominous area, especially on cloudy days. The old, rusted ski lifts are still there and look like they belong in an apocalyptic movie scene. There's also an old lookout tower that people love to walk to the top of. The views up there are phenomenal. Going up there when the autumn leaves are most colorful is one of my all-time favorite activities. Or, at least, it was.

I was in my early twenties when my friend, Christie (alias), invited me and our other friend, Mackenzie (alias), to sleep at the top of that tower in early fall. Technically, nobody was supposed to go up there at nighttime, but I don't know of anyone who ever got in trouble for doing so. The area I grew up in presented many opportunities for activities we weren't supposed to do but always got away with. That's probably because many of those acts are traditions, even for some police officers in my hometown.

So, they must ignore things that they could ticket people for.

I can't say it was the most appealing idea for me, for I tend to get unbearably cold relatively quickly, but it was Christie's wish. She had also recently gone through a devastating breakup, where she learned her ex-boyfriend had impregnated another girl that she already didn't get along with for unrelated reasons, so I felt obligated to do anything that might help ease her pain.

Camping in that old lookout tower didn't seem like something Christie would typically like to do, which made it apparent that she was determined to distract herself from the pain of her current reality. I suppose it's common for someone to crave adventure during and after intense heartache. A few years later, I learned that for myself firsthand.

Also, Christie had a brother who was only a couple of years older than us, and he was notorious for doing all sorts of daring things. He was a pretty happy, carefree kind of guy, and I believe she reached a point where his acts finally influenced her to step out of her comfort zone a bit. She must've concluded that he was going about his life the right way and that she would be less vulnerable to future heartbreak if she adopted his outlook.

The night we chose to sleep in the tower started with comfortable weather, but unfortunately, the temperature plummeted shortly after sundown. The three of us got into our sleeping bags and huddled them close to one another, almost like we were cuddling. That was a nice moment, and I felt Christie's appreciation for us having gone there with her. It probably reassured her that she had friends who would do pretty much anything for her—that there was no reason to feel lonely, no matter what her future presented. It was nice to hear Christie laugh for a change. Her aura during the few days leading up to that point seriously made me wonder if she would ever find humor in anything again.

But the mood turned when an odd screech paused our conversation.

The noise was followed by what sounded like an elephant charging through a nearby patch of the surrounding woods. It was so confusing how it just erupted out of nowhere. None of us heard any lead-up signs that a large animal was approaching. The noise ceased after a few seconds of the unidentified creature stomping through the trees. Several moments later, Mackenzie asked Christie and me if we had any ideas on what could've been responsible for those loud sounds. I was reluctant to reply because I assumed the culprit was still around us. I didn't suspect it had gone almost directly beneath us.

The first thing I saw was the wrack of antlers. Their size made me think that it had to be a bull moose, but the shape of the antlers was much closer to what you would see on a male deer. Initially, it was too dark to see the body, but I figured it was because the fur color was much darker than the antlers.

I was the first to glimpse it, and I whispered to the others a few moments later, informing them of what I saw. But there was a mysterious screech-like noise before either of my friends could respond, quickly followed by something smashing against the steel stairway. It was clear that whatever was down there had heard me and seemed not to like that we were up there. Something about that noise confirmed it wasn't a deer or moose down there. It sounded much more like a predator. But what kind of carnivore would have antlers? That was when I knew we were dealing with some freak of nature.

Mackenzie's eyes conveyed that she regretted agreeing to camp out there. To make matters worse, not one of us had brought anything out there that could be used as a weapon to defend ourselves. But I had a feeling that it didn't matter much anyway. Whatever was down there was too big to be affected by something like a pocket knife. I would've felt somewhat secure at that moment if we had a gun, but I don't think we had any firearms experience anyway.

The only thing that provided any comfort was that the creature looked too big to make its way up the steps. The staircase was quite narrow all the way to the top, forcing people who climbed it to go up and down it in a single-file line. If not for that, I probably would've already considered whether I would need to somehow climb down the tower's exterior to avoid the unidentified entity.

I'm unsure of their technical term, but there were little holes throughout the steel floor, enabling us to see bits of the creature.

"Oh my god," Mackenzie whispered. "What is that?"

Carefully, Christie and I leaned our heads over Mackenzie's legs to check where she was looking. I vividly remember getting such an uncomfortable knot in my throat and stomach when I saw a portion of the face staring up at us. It wasn't a human's face, but strangely, it was more human than anything else. I observed it enough to establish there was no snout.

The best way I can describe it would be to say that it was like a longer-than-average person's head, with antlers and no visible nose. Although it was difficult to get a good look at the eyes, for they constantly shifted their focus in various directions, they looked different from a human's. There was something very off about them. I've always believed that eyes are indeed the windows to the soul, and they hinted that this individual, whatever they were, was extremely sick.

Initially, my confused brain assumed that this had to be a mentally ill individual who lived in the woods, had lost their nose to an accident or birth defect, and walked around wearing deer antlers and a fur coat. I had heard rumors about strange sightings of various things in those woods but never took any of it seriously. I hadn't had any experiences with cryptids, supernatural entities, aliens, etc., so I guess my mind wasn't in a place to immediately assess that

that's what was trying to squeeze its way up the staircase. Although the size of the thing alone was terrifying, I remember feeling grateful that it didn't seem capable of making its way up those steps.

Christie wasn't as confident as I was that we were safe from the thing getting up there, so she grabbed some of the snacks lying on the platform near her sleeping bag and tossed them onto the ground. The granola bars fell near the entity, but it didn't seem interested or fazed. That was when I knew this thing was there for *us*. It was interested in meat.

"What should we do?" Mackenzie murmured, almost too frightened to speak. Neither I nor

Christie knew how to respond. We all felt like sitting ducks, awaiting this strange woodsman, animal, or whatever it was to figure out a way up there. If it could somehow squeeze its bulky body up those stairs, there wouldn't be much we could do to escape other than jump from the tower. But that would've been a leap of faith, for even if we somehow survived the fall, we were almost certain to break most of our bones. Then, we would be even more defenseless while waiting for the creature to confront us at ground level.

"What do you want with us?" I suddenly blurted out. But it didn't respond or even make a sound. "Go away! Get out of here!" I shouted several times, but the entity didn't seem to mind.

I feel terrible admitting this, but I recall hoping someone else would wander into the area to take the entity's attention away from us. Of course, I would never wish for anything bad to happen to innocent people, but I figured we would all devise an exit strategy. That seemed like the only possible way we would live to talk about that night and get answers regarding what we had encountered.

I'm unsure how much time had passed, but the entity spent quite a while trying to make its way up the stairs before another nearby noise caught its attention. It sounded like a few deer had detected what was in proximity after accidentally approaching our area and decided to take off before it was too late. I was still so focused on figuring out what we were dealing with that my analysis of anything else was probably off.

It's hard to say whether overwhelming fear strengthens or weakens your senses. I've read clashing opinions on that topic, so I'm unsure what to think. It probably depends on the individual, but it's difficult to envision anyone acting composed in that same situation. Although it was anything but a dream, it felt very dreamlike. I suppose that's because it seemed so bizarre to even be real in the first place.

I watched as the entity turned away from us above to gaze toward the commotion. That was when I saw its back and observed that the pair of antlers was not attached to any helmet; they were part of its skull. Its back appeared to be missing fur in various places, possibly due to an injury or disease. Whatever that was from, it made the creature look sick and malnourished. Could that be why it was interested in us in the first place? Could it have been so desperate for flesh that it needed to pursue humans?

Fortunately, whatever had run off through the thicket seemed more enticing for the strange creature trying to make its way up the steps. The timing was perfect, leading my friends and I to discuss whether it could've been a guardian angel looking out for us. Sometimes, I've even pondered whether that antlered creature was a physical manifestation of a demon and an angel made the noise to draw attention away from us. If and when you see stuff like what we encountered that night, you'll notice your mind races to create all sorts of possible explanations, no matter how illogical or unbelievable they might sound.

It took us a while to feel secure enough to walk down the steps, but we finally did and made it to our car without additional scares. The environment was so calm while we walked back there, almost making it feel like the heart-pounding incident never happened. If it weren't for having two friends with me to confirm that it did happen, I wonder if I would've tried to dismiss it as nothing more than my imagination.

I'll probably never get any indisputable answers for what we experienced that night, only theories. But I certainly appreciate books like yours, Tom, for they help people cope with unexplainable happenings. Sadly, there aren't many mainstream tools to assist others with the trauma that often follows such events. I never went to see a therapist, for they would probably attempt to convince me that the antlered entity was merely a figment of my imagination. That would bother me, so I've always steered clear.

I suspect we encountered a wendigo that night, and I believe those things are the physical manifestations of demons. There was something so sinisterly dark about its presence, and I hope never to cross paths with anything like it again.

Thank you for your time, and God bless.

To claim your free eBooks, visit

www.LivingAmongBigfoot.com

and click the FREE BOOKS tab!

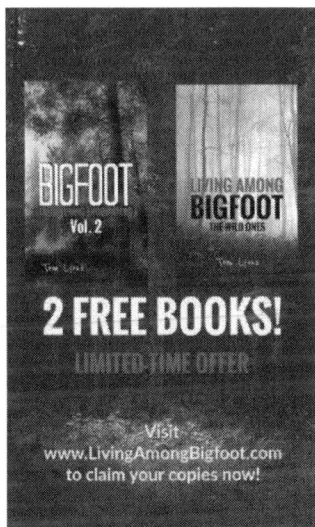

Report #3

Hey Tom, my name is Lera. I'm reaching out to share something that happened to me and my husband in 2016. Even though it's been a few years since the incident, there are occasions when it still feels fresh in my mind—usually when I wake up in the middle of the night and have trouble falling back asleep. When restless and

uncomfortable, my brain tends to
bring me back to those dark moments.

Neither of us had much money,
nor did our families, so we decided to
get hitched at a public beach in Santa
Barbara with just a handful of the
people we're closest to. It was a very
low-key celebration but a far more
special moment than I anticipated.
Unfortunately, that occasion was
immediately followed up by one of the
most unsettling events possible.

Since we didn't have much
money for a wedding, our options for a
honeymoon were somewhat limited.
My husband, Gustavo, had recently
purchased a camper to hitch to the
back of his pickup truck, for he had
recently quit his job and wanted to use

it to start his own business. He went back and forth many times on what type of business he wanted but ultimately settled on selling shaved ice because the expenses were relatively low. I was a bit nervous that our livelihood was about to depend on selling snow cones, but I was so in love with the guy that I was willing to overlook potential future struggles.

But since the guy had just spent most of his savings on his new investment, we devised the plan to kill two birds with one stone, using the camper on our honeymoon. Gustavo mapped out a beautiful route to travel up and down the West Coast, and we left early in the morning after our quaint but charming wedding. The road trip started in a very magical way, and everything felt right.

Although our funds were limited, it was hard to imagine the celebration having gone any better. I was on cloud nine at the beginning of that trip. That blissful sensation increased when we arrived at a Big Sur, California, wine bar overlooking the ocean's crashing waves. It was stunningly gorgeous, and I wouldn't trade those memories for anything. However, the next night, when we parked in the woods about ninety minutes north of Big Sur, we endured the scare of a lifetime. I'm still unsure what to think of what we experienced that night, for it altered my perception of the world around us.

It was around 10:30 PM when we heard the first noise. I remember glancing at the clock, thinking it was odd that someone would be walking around our campsite at that hour. But before jumping the gun, deciding that some psychopath was trespassing, I reminded myself that neither of us was familiar with the area. For all we knew, we might've parked in front of some secret path that leads to some late-night hangout spot. I hadn't seen many people around there while it was light outside, so the chances of us encountering a single weirdo seemed slim. There had to be a logical explanation.

But the strangest part about these footsteps was how, one second, they sounded like they were a solid ten yards away, but the next, they seemed just inches away from our shelter. That routine repeated several times, leaving us utterly confused. We figured it had to be a human out there, for the footsteps sounded bipedal. Because of that, we weren't considering any other possibility.

Judging by Gustavo's face, I could tell he was on the fence about whether to step outside to confront whoever was out there or if it was better to wait and hope the intruder got bored and wandered off.

"Should we announce we're about to call the police if they don't leave?" I whispered to Gustavo.

He held up his pointer finger, suggesting we keep quiet while trying to figure out what was happening. I suspect he thought it might be a state authority out there, gathering all the broken rules they could ticket us for. It's probably more accurate to say that's what he hoped for—a best-case scenario.

Suddenly, I nearly leaped out of my skin when it sounded like something slammed against the camper's outer wall—opposite where our gazes were directed. That was when it started to feel like someone was toying with us, and my husband couldn't hold off any longer.

"Who's out there?" Gustavo shouted, attempting to sound macho. I had only known him as a lowkey, relaxed man, so seeing him in that state was bizarre. I could still detect the shakiness in his voice, which made me feel even more creeped out. There's nothing like seeing the individual you consider your protector in an intimidated state. It made me feel so much more in danger—like things were on the brink of going terribly wrong.

I had hoped we would hear the sounds of footsteps running away as soon as Gustavo announced his awareness, but there was nothing. All there was was an eerie silence.

For a few more minutes, Gustavo and I did nothing but look at each other while listening carefully to the space outside our camper. I asked him if he thought whoever was out there had run off, but again, he held his pointer finger up, requesting that I remain quiet. I was desperate for anything that might bring me a sense of relief. I wanted to know that we would be okay and nobody planned to harm us. I had never felt such longing for that magnitude of reassurance, and that notion was terrifying.

Suddenly, there was a thud on the roof of our camper, followed by an irritating scratching-like noise. I couldn't tell whether something sharp was getting dragged along the metal or if something was walking across it. But it was worse than nails on a chalkboard. My recollection of that awkward noise gives me chills. That was when I thought maybe we weren't dealing with a human after all. It seemed absurd to suspect that a human could get onto the roof without a ladder. That was more like something a stealth animal like a panther would do.

I thought it was strange how the recognition that it must be an animal out there seemed to bring Gustavo a bit of comfort. I watched him breathe a sigh of relief. I'm not exactly sure how I felt about that realization. If there was any contrast, the possibility of a sharp-toothed large cat seemingly trying to get inside our camper was a little more terrifying than the alternative. I felt confident that a human wouldn't be able to get inside, but a strong and hungry animal is a different story. Of course, I had heard plenty of reports of wild animals so determined to find food that they ripped heavy-duty doors from the hinges. Some readers might find that fear a little silly, but it's not like I was a wildlife expert, so I had so much trouble ascertaining how I should feel.

In any case, I remember thanking myself for always locking doors, even when unnecessary. I did it automatically ever since my great-grandmother walked in on me sitting on the toilet when I was four or five years old. That was another traumatic experience.

I watched my husband as he began to get out of bed quietly. I didn't need to ask what he was doing to know he was heading toward the window that provided the most expansive view of the outside. It was probably too dark to see much of anything, but he probably just wanted to check for movement of any kind, which could indicate whether there was more than one of whatever animal could be out there.

"Anything?" I whispered, still in bed. He didn't respond immediately, which I took as a sign that something had grabbed his attention.

"I'm pretty sure I see someone standing behind a tree over there," he replied, pointing toward an area barely in view to the left. There was another thud on the roof immediately after he said that, raising the suspicion that more than one entity lurked around our campsite. But if Gustavo had indeed spotted a human peeking at us from behind a tree, what were they doing there while a ferocious animal roamed our roof? I was having so much trouble making sense of anything. All I knew for sure was that I wanted more than anything to be home.

Gustavo started tiptoeing away from the window after a few more peculiar noises atop our portable shelter. I watched him grab his phone to check to see if, by some chance, he had cellular reception. The look in his eyes suggested it was futile even to bother.

"What're we going to do?" I whispered with a trembling voice.

Gustavo didn't say anything, but I could tell he was considering going outside to try to intimidate whoever or whatever was out there.

"Don't," I said. "Please don't."

I remember feeling extremely cold in those moments. The temperature wasn't hot, but it wasn't chilly enough for me to feel like I needed to wrap myself in a hundred blankets. I didn't know enough about cryptozoology back then, so I didn't connect the dots that whatever was outside the camper could trigger such frigid sensations. At the time, I figured it was merely my trepidation of the situation that caused all that. My husband noticed my shaking, for he fetched another blanket from a drawer beneath the bed and wrapped it around me. As he did that, I observed that he was also trembling.

"I'm going to get us out of here," Gustavo whispered. Initially, I liked the sound of that idea, but I quickly realized that meant he would have to go outside to make his way into the truck. I suppose I wasn't quite accustomed to using the camper, so it took a moment for that frightening fact to dawn on me.

"No, I don't want you going out there!" I argued, shaking harder by the second.

Gustavo kissed me on the forehead in a way that suggested everything would be fine while simultaneously displaying his love just in case it was his final goodbye. I probably would've fought harder to prevent him from leaving the camper had I not been in such a troubled state myself. It's impressive what terror can do to you. I was so focused on trying to track whatever was outside that I was barely considering what was going on inside. Before I knew it, Gustavo was already halfway out the door.

I was so relieved when I heard the truck door slamming shut, indicating he made it without getting attacked. But then I heard an awful scream piercing the calm night air. Though it was difficult to tell which direction it had come from, that brought me back to thinking it was merely a group of trespassing humans. It sounded so ladylike, only more guttural—like something a female demon would do if startled. The longer the noise continued, the more uncomfortable it became. It was almost like its frequency was toxic to my ears.

I almost cried joyfully when the camper started moving, indicating that Gustavo was safely driving us out of there. It was almost hard to wrap my head around the concept we had escaped, and that horrifying experience would soon become a piece of the past. Although the ominous screams continued, I could no longer hear anything atop the roof. And it seemed like whoever was causing the screaming was getting further and further away as if they were watching us leave the area.

Suddenly, it felt like we had collided with a wall, causing me to stumble and fall onto my face. There wasn't any loud crashing noise, so I was confident we couldn't have collided with another vehicle. Then I started to worry if maybe we had hit a tree. What if Gustavo had gotten injured on his way to the truck, leaving him unable to drive? Even though I was already terrified, the idea of something like that happening to my husband made me feel like I was on the verge of a heart attack. As I pride myself off the camper floor, I try to take deep breaths to regain even an ounce of calm. I started hoping Gustavo had stomped on the brakes because he saw something strange ahead and didn't want to run into it. That was, of course, the best-case scenario I could come up with.

Not long after I rose to my feet, the irritating pitch of the truck's horn started going off repeatedly. What was Gustavo honking at? Was there someone in the way attempting to block our exit? But then I also heard my husband stepping on the accelerator. Were we caught in a ditch, and he couldn't get us out? But that wouldn't explain why he simultaneously laid his hand down on the horn.

"Get out of here!" Gustavo started shouting in between honks. "Get the hell out of there!"

His voice conveyed that he was trying to overcome immense fear. Who was he talking to? Of course, no human was strong enough to prevent our truck from moving forward. That was when I thought someone had to have pulled their vehicle in front of ours, preventing us from leaving. I figured it had to be a police officer about to ticket us for trying to spend the night somewhere we weren't supposed to. Well, that was what my mind wanted to think.

Desperate for confirmation that my wacky theory was correct, I peeked my head out the door. Immediately, it felt like I had been transported to another world occupied by manlike beasts. These *things*, whatever they were, pushed against the front of our vehicle. It appeared they had lifted it just high enough off the ground to where the front tires couldn't touch the ground. It took me several moments to comprehend that there were three of them before our vehicle. Initially, it looked like one massive clump of tangled hair. I was knowledgeable enough to know California no longer hosted a grizzly bear population.

I NEARLY LOST MY MIND when I saw the long muscular arms,

complete with hands and opposable thumbs. Although they didn't look too much like anything I had ever seen before, I would have to say they most closely resembled orangutans. But their fur appeared much darker— more like a chimpanzee's. It was the freakiest sight I had ever laid eyes upon. There are no words to justify just how disturbed I was.

I could hear the beasts panting while they continued attempting to prevent our vehicle from progressing. Gustavo kept pressing the accelerator and honking the horn, apparently confident that the humanlike beasts would eventually grow too exhausted, even with their remarkable strength and endurance. Fortunately, none of the creatures seemed to pay any attention to me. But then I wondered whether that would change if they found a way to prevent our truck from going anywhere. More chills ran down my spine, and I remember nearly losing my balance and falling out of the camper. I don't even want to imagine what would've happened had I not caught myself and closed the door.

While crouching nervously inside the portable shelter, I awaited more ear-piercing yelps, ready to muffle my ears. But they never came. I suspect the beasts had grown too exhausted from trying to stop our motor vehicle. Maybe they can't unleash that horrible noise when they're short of breath. Of course, that was merely another theory, but it seemed logical.

The commotion became so chaotic and overwhelming, and I couldn't think of anything to do except sit with my back against the wall and my head and arms resting on my knees. I prayed for the mayhem to end and for us to return home and live our newlywed lives peacefully.

It wasn't long before there was a loud thud, and we began moving again. "Holy shit," I muttered, more relieved than ever. I even wondered if I had died and gone to Heaven. Better yet, my husband was no longer slapping the horn, causing me to suspect that there were no more psychotic manlike beasts in our path. At least, none that he could see.

When the bumpy ride turned into a smooth one, I felt relaxed enough to stand up and glance out the window. As I had hoped, we had made it onto a road. I can't even express how good it felt to see headlights from other vehicles. That helped reassure me we were far out of the reach of whatever the hell those things were that we had just encountered.

Gustavo turned into a gas station parking lot twenty minutes or so later. Although stepping out of the camper still felt weird, nothing could delay me from thanking my husband for his bravery. I had never been so happy to feel myself in his arms, and I'm still convinced that that moment strengthened our marriage in ways that few other things could. I found myself weeping tears of joy into his chest. It was difficult to believe that we had made it out of that nightmare alive.

"What on God's green earth were those things?" I said between sobs.

"Pretty sure that was Bigfoot," Gustavo replied. "Or rather *Bigfeet,* I should say, since there was more than one of them."

"I can't believe those things are real. They were right there in front of our truck."

"That they were," Gustavo sighed. His voice indicated he was just as shocked as I was that we made it out of there intact.

"What do you think those things would've done to us had they trapped us there?" I asked.

"Let's go find a motel and run ourselves a warm bath," Gustavo said while rubbing my back, deciding it was best to avoid such grim thoughts. I understood why he didn't want to talk about it, especially at that time, but a part of me will forever wonder what those creatures do to the people they capture. I hate to admit it, but I suspect they want our meat. I highly doubt such an elusive animal would go anywhere near humans unless for sustenance. Imagining what we saw munching away on human flesh is one of the most vile things I can think of. Although they clearly weren't human like you or I, there's still a hint of cannibalism somewhere in there. I can't help but wonder if there's something to that.

My husband reported our experience to the BFRO (Bigfoot Field Researchers Organization), but I don't think he ever heard back from any of its associates. Maybe there's a chance the Email landed in their spam folder. But that's how I stumbled upon your sasquatch books. It was while I was searching for a worthy place to document our story. More of the public needs to know of this kind of stuff. I don't think it's acceptable that so many go near the woods without knowing the entire range of risks.

Visit My Digital Book Store

If you're looking for NEW reads, check out my digital store, www.TomLyonsBooks.com.

Buying my books directly from me means you save money—because my store will always sell for less than big retailers. My store also offers sales, deals, bundles, and pre-order discounts you won't find anywhere else.

Visit my store now to get a FREE audiobook!

Report #4

Lost Rivers State Park is the name of the location in West Virginia where it all happened. Considering the horror that occurred while my girlfriend and I tried to unwind and get a healthy dose of nature, it's a suitable title. I think humans enjoy going into the woods so much because there is a risk factor—an element of danger that relieves our minds from the daily grind that most experience in modern times.

I brought my girlfriend, Jen, who is now my wife, on a camping trip to the state park because I initially had planned to ask her to marry me. Well, that grand plan got obliterated after we ended up in a situation that has kept us away from the woods ever since. It bent our perception of what exists in our world, and I sometimes wish that wasn't the case. I miss wandering the forest. We both do. Jen and I first met online in 2017 and went on a hike in Tennessee for our first date. We had such a great time following our introduction that we decided to visit all the best hiking trails in the area. That was how we started spending a lot of time together and discovered that we have many of the same interests, most of which involved the outdoors.

One thing led to the next, and we soon found ourselves embarking on extensive road trips that took us to what had to be many of our country's top campgrounds. Early in our relationship, there was a period that must've been around five or six weeks straight of us staying at a different campground every weekend. Those are some of my best memories that I'll treasure forever. It's such a shame that those adventures had to cease. People close to us have suggested we get back out there, but they don't seem to understand that we would never be able to relax in the woods, especially at night. I don't think it's possible for anyone who hasn't encountered strange things in the woods to truly relate to how we have felt ever since the event.

I can't blame them, for I firmly believe I wouldn't be able to either beforehand. Sadly, I probably would've been one of the first to dismiss anyone claiming to have gone through that sort of thing. That's not to say I would've ridiculed them, but I don't think I could've taken the claim seriously. Hearing about something similar to what we went through would've sounded too delusional.

Jen and I arrived at Lost Rivers State Park in early June 2019. I recall feeling so grateful for the weather. It couldn't have been more perfect.

But that first evening, while snuggling before the campfire, we heard a woman calling out someone's name. She sounded distressed. Jen and I got up to meet her near the edge of our campsite, and she informed us that she was searching for her twelve-year-old daughter. She didn't seem excessively worried, like I had initially thought. The woman explained she wanted to find her daughter before deciding what to cook, but it wasn't uncommon for her to wander off. She made some remarks about how her daughter had already started going through her angsty preteen stage and that she now preferred to be alone as much as possible. The woman seemed more frustrated than worried, but that was only the beginning.

We asked the lady if she wanted us to help her in the search, but she insisted that it wasn't necessary and that Jen and I should get back to enjoying our evening. She apologized for disturbing us and got on with her search. Soon, the woman was out of hearing distance, and we resumed snuggling in front of the campfire with our bottle of wine. I was maybe about fifteen minutes away from the time I originally had planned to whip out the engagement ring when what sounded like a young girl's voice called out for someone.

It had probably been almost an hour since we encountered the woman searching for her daughter. We heard the voice again a few minutes later. It was difficult to ascertain whether it indicated fear, pain, or both, but I knew we had to check things out.

Strangely, the voice seemed to be getting further away the closer we got. We called out a few times, but I didn't sense that it was responding to us. It almost seemed to disregard us entirely. Another peculiar aspect was how the voice seemed to be moving in the opposite direction of where the lady had come from earlier. I wasn't sure where the woman had set up camp. I imagined it was a considerable distance away, given that we hadn't heard the faintest noise of conversation from any direction.

"Hello? Do you need help?" Jen and I called out several times while tracking the voice, but it never replied. It never sounded like anyone was annunciating a word. If anything, it was more like a whimper, which made things far more alarming. I couldn't think of why a twelve-year-old girl would be whimpering from fear or pain had she been beside her mother. I figured she still had to be lost, but why wouldn't her mother still search for her? We hadn't heard anyone else calling for their child since we first encountered the woman. We kept following the noise, somewhat aimlessly, eventually realizing that we might have veered too far from camp because we were unfamiliar with the area.

"Do you think we should go back?" Jen asked, having lost confidence that we would pinpoint where the mysterious whimpers came from. I told her I would escort her back to camp but felt responsible for keeping searching in case someone truly needed help. She rejected the offer, agreeing that I was right to want to keep looking. I'm unsure if we would have felt obligated to leave our camp had it not been for the lack of people in the vicinity. Aside from the woman we met earlier and whoever was making the whimpers, it seemed we were the only ones around. I had intended to venture to a place where I could expect privacy, but I had no idea it would be *that* private.

Things got creepier when we found a pair of childlike sneakers lying on the ground about ten feet apart. Although they were used shoes, they didn't appear to have been left outside for days. If that were the case, the elements would've done a number on them. That was when things started to feel very wrong, affirming that we were dealing with a child lost in the surrounding woods. But why hadn't we heard the mother's calls since crossing paths with her earlier?

"Hello? Does someone need help?" Jen suddenly blurted out. I wasn't sure why, but breaking the silence felt like a bad idea—like we should refrain from drawing attention our way. A few moments later, I learned why.

Jen and I looked at each other when a loud, menacing hiss echoed throughout the area. Whatever had made the noise sounded way too close for comfort. Her eyes conveyed instant regret over having announced our presence.

"Let's get back to camp," I whispered once the mysterious hissing dissipated.

Jen nodded without uttering another word.

Holding hands, we turned around and headed toward our destination. I didn't say anything, for I didn't want to make my girlfriend more scared than she already was, but I didn't recognize where we were. We passed an old trail sign that wasn't readable, and I just knew I would've noticed it when passing it before. Reluctant to stop our stride, which might hint to Jen that I wasn't certain of our location, I continued moving us forward, hoping it wouldn't be long before we spotted our campsite ahead. A few minutes later, it became even more apparent that I didn't recognize our surroundings.

"Are we lost?" Jen whispered, confirming that I wasn't the only one wondering whether we had made a wrong turn. I tried to think of an appropriate response when I noticed a strange glow between trees in the distance.

"That must be the child's mother," I whispered, thankful for a reason to change the subject.

Jen and I continued moving forward, relieved we were about to interact with another human who could help us realize where we were. Although the light was orange like a fire, it had a fainter flow and wasn't moving the way the flames of a fire move. But I didn't think too hard about that at the time. All I could think about was that we were about to speak with another person who would be able to assist with directions back to camp.

Like the previous whimpers, the strange glow seemed to get further away with every step we took toward it. Eventually, it got to a point where I assumed it had to be someone carrying a flashlight or some device that helped them to better see in the dark.

"Hello? Are you looking for someone?" I called out, but there was no response. The light quickly faded away and reappeared a few moments later, maybe thirty to forty feet from where it was before. It reminded me of a firefly's glow, only substantially larger.

"I want to go home," Jen murmured, signaling she had a bad feeling. I felt a similar sensation, but I didn't want to admit that to her or myself. I thought there had to be a practical explanation for whatever was happening, and there was no reason to feel as unsettled as I was.

Silently, we stood in place while the ominous glow repeated the same routine of vanishing and reappearing to the right until it had completed a full clockwise circle around us.

"What's going on?" Jen murmured after it had finished making its way around us. It was apparent she was terrified by that point, and I was doing everything possible not to let the mysterious phenomenon overwhelm me. I had to keep it together to keep us both safe from the potential danger.

"C'mon, I think camp is this way," I said, unsure of what else to say, for I couldn't explain what was happening. I had never seen anything like it.

Suddenly, I heard the whimpering again, but this time, it came from what sounded like only several yards behind us. I'll never forget that dreadful moment as I began turning my head to look behind us. Jen shrieked before I could even lay eyes on the scene. That was all I needed to confirm I was about to gaze upon something horrible.

At first sight, I had trouble understanding what I was looking at. There were three individuals behind me—two of whom were present against their will. I couldn't help but internally deny the horror, for it was simply too incomprehensible that anyone could commit such an awful act.

A cloaked entity stood hunched before a fire, tending to what looked like a large circle pot or pan that didn't have a handle. Behind the creepy cloaked individual were two females, side by side, hanging from a tree branch by their feet. I immediately noticed I couldn't see rope or anything needed to secure them to the wood, which I couldn't make sense of. In any case, I right away understood why I hadn't heard the mother searching for her child after we encountered her the first time. It was because the cloaked individual had captured both her and her daughter.

None of the three before us seemed to acknowledge us in any way. And I discovered why when I attempted to rush toward the young girl and mother to help them down from the tree. I only made it a few yards before running into an invisible barrier. It wasn't like running into a hard wall, but more like soft, bendable glass—or maybe more like fully transparent rubber. I also noticed a faint warmth radiating from it, but that could've just been because I was closer to the fire.

I then hollered at the cloaked individual, demanding they release the woman and her daughter. But they didn't turn to look my way. I wasn't even sure whether they heard me or chose to ignore me. It almost felt like I was watching a movie, for nobody at the scene acknowledged my presence.

"No!" I shouted as the child began hovering toward the cloaked figure with her arms and legs spread and her back aimed toward the ground. Although her eyes appeared about halfway open, she wasn't behaving like she was awake and trying to free herself. And that was when I realized that she was either unconscious or unable to move a muscle due to something the cloaked individual did to her. The mother wasn't moving a muscle either, but her back was turned toward the scene, so I couldn't see her eyes or know if she was even aware of what was happening. I only knew it was the woman we had spoken to earlier because I recognized the outfit.

I continued shouting and banging my fists against the transparent barrier while the fire grew larger until I couldn't see anything other than flames on the other side. Suddenly, the fire vanished in a flash before Jen and I found ourselves back at our campsite, still standing in the same positions. The atmosphere became dead silent, and there was no sign of the three individuals anywhere in sight.

My heart pounded as I looked in every direction. I wasn't even listening to my girlfriend's questions, for I was still too focused on wanting to help the child and her mother. I have no idea how or why we encountered that nasty scene before somehow being transported back to our campsite. If Jen hadn't been there to confirm every aspect of what I saw, I might have assumed I had gone insane briefly, and none of that dreadful scene actually occurred.

We packed everything up as quickly as possible and drove out of there. I wanted to help the mother and child, but even if I somehow stumbled upon that horrific scene again, I knew there was nothing I would be able to do. It felt like I would be doing nothing but putting Jen back in danger. If anything happened to her, but I somehow lived, I never would've been able to forgive myself.

Whatever it was we saw that night, it was undoubtedly supernatural. But it also felt satanic. I wish it weren't the case, but I know that the cloaked individual intended to cook the child and mother in that fire that grew before our eyes. I deeply regret that Jen had to witness something of that evil nature. Of course, I had no way of knowing we would encounter anything remotely like that, but I still felt guilty. Neither of us could establish how to even go about reporting something so bizarre, and this report is pretty much the first time we did.

Not a day passes without me wishing I could wipe my memory of that disturbing incident.

Conclusion

Thanks for reading! If you want more, read *Camping Horror Stories: Volume 3.*

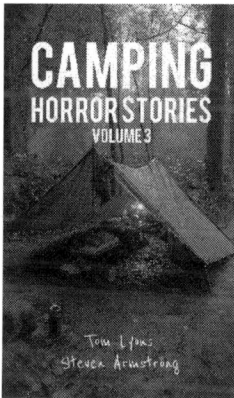

Editor's Note

Before you go, I'd like to say "thank you" for purchasing this book.

I know you had various cryptid-related books to choose from, but you took a chance at my content.
Therefore, thanks for reading this one and sticking with it to the last page.

At this point, I'd like to ask you for a *tiny* favor; it would mean the world if you could leave a review wherever you purchased this book.

Your feedback will aid me in creating products you and many others can enjoy.

Mailing List Sign-Up Form

Don't forget to sign up for the newsletter email list. I promise I will not use it to spam you but to ensure you always receive the first word on any new releases, discounts, or giveaways! All you need to do is visit the following URL and enter your email address.

URL-

http://eepurl.com/dhnspT

Social Media

Feel free to follow/reach out to me with questions or concerns on either Instagram or Twitter! I will do my best to follow back and respond to all comments.

Instagram:

@living_among_bigfoot

Twitter:

@AmongBigfoot

About the Editor

A simple man at heart, Tom Lyons lived an ordinary existence for his first 52 years. Native to the great state of Wisconsin, he went through the motions of everyday life, residing near his family and developing a successful online business. The world he once knew would completely change shortly after moving out west, where he was confronted by the allegedly mythical species known as Bigfoot.

You can email him directly at:

Living.Among.Bigfoot@gmail.com

Printed in Great Britain
by Amazon

31625830R00065